K M A Ahamed Zubair

Arabic Prose Literature and Its Development in Tamil Nadu

K M A Ahamed Zubair

Arabic Prose Literature and Its Development in Tamil Nadu

Notable Arabic Prose Authors and their Works of Tamil Nadu

Noor Publishing

Imprint
Any brand names and product names mentioned in this book are subject to trademark, brand or patent protection and are trademarks or registered trademarks of their respective holders. The use of brand names, product names, common names, trade names, product descriptions etc. even without a particular marking in this work is in no way to be construed to mean that such names may be regarded as unrestricted in respect of trademark and brand protection legislation and could thus be used by anyone.

Cover image: www.ingimage.com

Publisher:
Noor Publishing
is a trademark of
Dodo Books Indian Ocean Ltd. and OmniScriptum S.R.L publishing group

120 High Road, East Finchley, London, N2 9ED, United Kingdom
Str. Armeneasca 28/1, office 1, Chisinau MD-2012, Republic of Moldova, Europe
Printed at: see last page
ISBN: 978-620-7-47870-5

Arabic Prose Literature and Its Development in Tamil Nadu

Notable Arabic Prose Authors and their Works of Tamil Nadu

Dr.K.M.A.Ahamed Zubair

Associate Professor of Arabic, The New College, Chennai 600 014, India

اللغة العربية تحمل كلمة الله، وروح محمد ﷺ، وسر الإسلام،

This work has been dedicated to the Indian Islamic Missionaries (1500-1800)

Preface

The state of Tamil Nadu in India has a rich history of producing scholars, writers, jurists, hadith scholars, and interpreters whose works have gained acclaim across the Islamic world. The significance of their contributions to the Arabic language and Islamic sciences cannot be overstated. This collection of works and their authors highlights the depth of engagement with Arabic literature and Islamic thought in Tamil Nadu, showcasing the enduring legacy of these scholars.

Arabic, traditionally studied as the language of Islamic scholarship, has been nurtured and preserved in Tamil Nadu through the efforts of dedicated scholars and writers. These individuals have made significant strides in promoting and developing the language across various fields, including history, linguistics, Islamic jurisprudence, and literature. The establishment of numerous religious schools, Arabic colleges, Islamic institutes, and universities throughout the state has facilitated the spread of Arabic education and scholarship.

The advent of printing presses and the publication of

Arabic periodicals and magazines in Tamil Nadu further catalyzed the proliferation of Arabic literary works. These factors combined have led to a remarkable output of Arabic texts that not only serve educational purposes but also contribute to the global Islamic literary heritage.

This compilation focuses on a selection of Arabic works from Tamil Nadu that have gained widespread acceptance and recognition both within the state and beyond its borders. The range of subjects covered is vast, reflecting the diverse interests and expertise of Tamil Nadu's scholars. From historical treatises to linguistic manuals, and from Islamic jurisprudence to poetic translations, the works presented here are testament to the vibrant intellectual culture of Tamil Nadu.

In the domain of history, the detailed accounts of Arab contributions to modern and contemporary literature, the Mughal rule in India, and the historical connections between India and the Arab world are noteworthy. Linguistically, the effort to simplify and teach Arabic grammar and language, especially for non-native speakers, is commendable. The works in Islamic sciences, including elucidations of Quranic verses and Hadith, provide valuable insights and guidance for students and scholars alike.

Moreover, the biographies and hagiographies of prominent figures demonstrate the cultural and intellectual bridges built by Tamil Nadu scholars. Their dedication to preserving and expanding the Arabic language and Islamic knowledge is evident in the meticulous research and thoughtful writing that characterize their works.

This preface serves as an introduction to the rich tapestry of Arabic literature and Islamic scholarship from Tamil Nadu. It is hoped that this collection will inspire further study and appreciation of the contributions made by Tamil Nadu's scholars to the wider Islamic world. The intellectual heritage of this region is a source of pride and a testament to the enduring power of knowledge and cultural exchange.

Dr K M A Ahamed Zubair

Contents

Preface	03-05
Contents	06
The Arabs, Islam, and the Arabic Language in the State of Tamil Nadu	07-14
Prominent Arabic Prose Writers of Tamil Nadu	15-33
Prominent Arabic Prose Wriings of Tamil Nadu	34-47
Bibliography	48-53

The Arabs, Islam, and the Arabic Language in the State of Tamil Nadu

The state of Tamil Nadu is one of the renowned historical states located in southern India. Tamil Nadu is situated at the southernmost part of India, covering an area of 133,038 square kilometers. It is bordered to the east by the Bay of Bengal, to the west by the state of Kerala, to the north by the states of Andhra Pradesh and Karnataka, and to the south by Sri Lanka and the Indian Ocean. History bears clear witness to the close ties and relationships between the Arabs and Indians since ancient times. There have been various connections and relations between the Arabs and India since ancient times, even during the era of the Prophet Muhammad (peace be upon him), in trade, living, and religion.

Tamil Muslims have historically held a respectable place for their contributions in all fields. It is well known that the Tamil people were not only the first to engage with Arab traders even centuries before Islam, but also their conversion to Islam preceded any other group in this region. The brotherly relationship and friendly connection between the Arabs and the people of Tamil Nadu have been strong since a very long time ago, even before the time of Jesus Christ (peace be upon him). The beauty of Tamil Nadu and its natural landscapes greatly impressed the Arabs. They would export Tamil Nadu's products, especially pepper, ginger, cloves, agarwood, musk, pearls, rubies, and coral, to distant lands like Yemen and the Levant. Some of them married Tamil Nadu women and settled in the coastal areas, blending their culture and civilization with the traditions and customs of Tamil Nadu, becoming an inseparable part of its culture.

Tamil Nadu was the first state to be visited by the Arabs. It was honored with the advent of Islam during the era of the noble Prophet (peace be upon him). The residents and rulers warmly welcomed the Arabs, embracing Islam and taking pride in it. The Arabic language has deeply and extensively influenced the people of Tamil Nadu, as well as other languages in India. Arabic permeated Tamil Nadu and flourished in its fertile environment. The relationship between the people of Tamil Nadu and Arab traders opened new horizons for the exchange of ideas, thoughts, and the understanding of cultures and languages.

The Arabic language and its literature have always been a focal point of interest for Muslims from this state since ancient times until today. It has never been considered a foreign or unfamiliar language to them. Arabic studies have been ongoing in Tamil Nadu since ancient times, a fact evidenced by the countless colleges and official universities across the state. Tamil Nadu has made significant contributions to the preservation, dissemination, and authorship of Arabic studies. The Arabic language has earned a prestigious position among the world's languages, not only because of its religious significance, which endears it to Muslims, but also due to the contributions of Arab and Islamic civilization.

The close relationships between this state and Arab countries, both in terms of homeland and people, continue to strengthen daily in various political, economic, and industrial fields. In this context, the study of the Arabic language plays a crucial role in enabling and fortifying these relationships. Arabic words have significantly blended into the Tamil language, with many people in this state believing that Arabic words are actually Tamil. Some of these words include: "وكيل" (agent), "سؤال" (question), "أصل" (origin), "نقل" (transport), "عطر" (perfume), "عنبر" (amber), "نفر" (individual), "شرط" (condition), "إنعام" (blessing), and "بديل" (alternative).

The Islamic thinker and Arab scholar, Sheikh Syed Abul Hasan Ali Hasani Nadwi, may Allah have mercy on him, said: "One of the manifestations of Muslim influence on

Indian culture and civilization is the influence of the Arabic language, which they brought to this land, in Indian languages, dialects, literature, and civilization. Muslims in South India—Madras, Kerala, and the Malabar region—have been very active in spreading religious and civil education, establishing Arabic religious schools and Islamic colleges."

The traveler Sheikh Muhammad bin Abdullah, known as Ibn Battuta (1303-1377 CE), visited this state and Serendib (Sri Lanka) during the era of King Aryachakravarthy. Ibn Battuta visited the town of Fattan in Tamil Nadu when Sultan Ghiyathuddin ruled Madurai. He mentioned his meeting with Sheikh Muhammad al-Naysaburi in this mentioned town.

Some Indian historians believe that Islam came to India after the conquest by Muhammad bin Qasim al-Thaqafi, who was sent by Al-Hajjaj bin Yusuf al-Thaqafi to conquer Sindh in northern India in 92 AH / 712 CE, or after several conquests by Mahmud of Ghazni in India. These views are incorrect and lack appropriate evidence. The truth is that Islam entered the southern coastal regions of India a century or more before these conquests. Islam was well-established in southern India since the time of the Prophet Muhammad (peace be upon him), as the relationship and connection between the Arabs and India were very ancient.

Arab and Indian Muslim preachers, imbued with the spirit of Islam, made effective efforts for the cause of Islam. These efforts began in Tamil Nadu before the first Islamic conquest by Muhammad bin Qasim al-Thaqafi around 91 AH in northern India. Islam entered from the eastern coasts of India in the Indian Ocean and from the western coasts in the Arabian Sea.

The companion Tamim al-Dari (may Allah be pleased with him) came to southern India and passed away there. His grave is currently in the village of "Kovallam," about thirty kilometers from the city of Madras (Chennai). This village, "Kovallam," is located on the shore of the Bay of Bengal and is a small village with an old-style mosque known as Malik bin Dinar Mosque. People from all over Tamil Nadu visit the grave of Sheikh Tamim al-Dari. There is another shrine on the shore of the Bay of Bengal, believed to be the shrine of the companion Ukkasha (may Allah be pleased with him). There is also a port named "Mahmud Bandar" on this coast. Ukkasha (may Allah be pleased with him) participated in the Battle of Badr and came to Tamil Nadu to spread the call of Islam. He was buried in "Mahmud Bandar," which the Portuguese later renamed "Port Nova."

Sultan Sayyid Ibrahim Shahid came from Medina by the order of the Prophet (peace be upon him) (in his dream) with his troops to spread Islam in Sindh in 557 AH / 1161 CE. Sheikh Sayyid Ibrahim (1135-1199 CE) was born in Medina and was a descendant of the Prophet Muhammad (peace be upon him). He came to southern India during the time of the Pandya Sultanate in 582 AH / 1186 CE and established an Islamic Sultanate with its capital at Pavithramanicka Pattanam (now known as Kilakarai). Sultan Sayyid Ibrahim was martyred in 595 AH / 1193 CE and ruled this region for twelve years.

Sultan Sayyid Ibrahim Shahid was buried in "Erwadi," and his grave remains there in the village to this day. These pieces of evidence indicate the religious ties between the Arabs and Tamil Nadu since the era of the Prophet Muhammad (peace be upon him). We have well-documented accounts and artifacts, including a small mosque near the Fort Railway Station in Trichnopoly. The mosque's foundational plaque names its builder as Haji Anwaruddin bin Haji Abdullah, and it was constructed in 738 CE (114 AH). This mosque is the oldest in India, predating even the Malik bin Dinar Mosque.

The Nawayati family and the Sheikh Sadaqatullah family

from Tamil Nadu are comparable to the Shah Waliullah family of Delhi in their role in spreading religious knowledge. They played a significant role in promoting the Arabic language throughout the region, dedicating their utmost efforts to this cause. These notable figures from Tamil Nadu made substantial contributions to the Islamic world with their scholarly works. Some of their renowned writings include:

1. "Al-Qasida Al-Witriyya" by Sheikh Madihur Rasul Sadaqatullah (1042-1115 AH), which comprises 4,210 verses.
2. "Milad al-Sami fi Mada'ih al-Nabi al-Tihami" by Sheikh Sam Shihabuddin (1045-1121 AH).
3. "Umda al-Hajjaj" by Sheikh Salahuddin (1051-1098 AH), a famous book detailing the rituals of Hajj and how to perform them with clear and simple expressions.
4. "Qasida Allaf al-Alif" and "Ilahi Kam Tubaqqini" by Sheikh Umar Wali (1162-1216 AH).
5. "Ahmadullah" by Sheikh Abdul Qadir Takya Sahib al-Kabir (1191-1272 AH).
6. "Al-Qasida al-Shafiya" by Sheikh Abdul Qadir Takya Sahib al-Saghir (1192-1267 AH), which contains 3,920 verses.

7. "Minhat Serendib fi Madih al-Habib" by Sheikh Syed Muhammad Imam al-Arous (1232-1312 AH).

These works reflect the significant literary and scholarly contributions of Tamil Nadu to the Islamic heritage, and their impact resonates throughout the Muslim world.

Prominent Figures of Arabic Prose in the State of Tamil Nadu

Qadi Irtiza Ali Khan Sahib, author of Nafais al-Irtizaiya (1198 AH - 1270 AH / 1783 - 1854 CE):

He was born in Kupam in 1198 AH, the son of Maulvi Mustafa Ali Khan Bahadur. He studied logic, philosophy, and metaphysics under the supervision of Maulana Haidar Ali, and learned Islamic sciences from Maulvi Muhammad Ibrahim Malibari, and Sufism from Sayyid Shah Ghulam Nasir al-Din Saadi al-Bulgrami. He spent his life with his father, engaged in studying Arabic and Persian and writing. He was appointed as the state's Mufti by the Nawab in 1230 AH / 1815 CE, and served for five years before resigning. His notable works in Arabic include:

a. Al-Tasrih fi al-Mantiq

b. Hashiyah Zahidiyah on al-Risalah

c. Hashiyah Sidrah al-Qatiyah

d. Sharh Jalaliyyah

e. Al-Minha al-Sara' fi al-Du'a

f. Al-Nafais al-Irtizaiya Sharh al-Kashif al-Dara'

g. Al-Tahdhib

Amir al-Din Husayn al-Waiz al-Wailuri:

He was a pious man, excelling in preaching and guidance, taught by Maulvi Akbar Sahib. His significant Arabic works include:

h. Uswah Hasanah fi Majalis al-Wa'z
i. Al-Sayf al-Qati' fi Radd Wahhabiyya
j. Radd al-Abatil li Ahl al-Anajil
k. Mumtaz al-Riwayah fi Ilm al-Fiqh

Maulvi Mufti Mahmoud (1269 AH - 1345 AH / 1853 - 1926 CE):

He was born the son of Qadi Badr al-Dawlah on the 25th of Rabi' al-Awwal 1269 AH. He learned Arabic, Persian, and Urdu, and traveled to various parts of India, debating contemporary scholars. He then went to Egypt, where he learned from many scholars. He spent his life in reading, writing, and teaching, and was awarded the Majidi Medal in 1879 CE by the Ottoman Caliphate. Mufti Mahmoud was skilled in mathematics and astronomy, preparing timetables for prayers, sunrise, sunset, fasting, and breaking fast. People sought his expertise for determining the Qibla direction for mosques. He passed away in 1345 AH / 1927 CE and was buried in the mosque of Walajah in Madras. His notable Arabic works include:

1. Asma' al-Rijal
2. Tashrih al-Ma'ani li Hifz
3. Al-Tashrih li al-Talwih
4. Al-Amani
5. Tanbih al-Muftun fi al-Firar
6. Al-Jawharah al-Saniyyah fi Tahqiq al-Niyyah
7. Hashiyah 'ala al-Ta'un
8. Hashiyah 'ala Nukhbat al-Fikr
9. Risalah fi Ilm al-Hay'ah
10. Al-Hizb al-Afham fi Manqabat al-Ghawth al-A'zam
11. Risalah fi al-Manaahi
12. Risalah fi Qada' al-Sawm
13. Al-Silk al-Mu'azzam 'ala al-Durr al-Munazzam
14. Sharh Hashiyah Abdullah
15. Fatwa fi al-Arbab
16. Al-Mutammimah fi Sharh Yazidi
17. Mir'at Awqat al-Qiblah
18. Al-Mujaddidiyyah

19. Al-Yatima

20. Al-Maqamah al-Badriyyah fi Milad Khayr al-Bariyyah

Abdul Ali "Assi" al-Madrasi (d. 1327 AH / 1909 CE):

His father was Mustafa al-Hanafi al-Chitturi al-Madrasi. He was one of the prominent scholars in grammar and language in Tamil Nadu, achieving proficiency in editing, annotation, writing, and poetry. His works include:

1. Tabsirat al-Hikmah fi Hifz
2. Al-Tabsirah al-Nizamiyyah
3. Takmilat Wajib al-Hifz
4. Tanbih al-Wahhabiyyin
5. Al-Ru'ūs al-Thamāniyyah
6. Mizan al-Lisan
7. Halla al-Tasārīf al-Mushkilah

Abdullah al-Madrasi (1205 AH - 1267 AH / 1791 - 1851 CE)

This noble prince was born on the 27th of Sha'ban, 1205

AH, and studied under the skilled scholars of his time. He served as a commander in the army of the Amir of Madras for a period. He died in 1267 AH and was buried in the old mosque of Madras. His notable contributions include:

1. Al-Durr al-Thamin fi Sharh al-Arba'in li al-Nawawi
2. A book on the men of Sahih Muslim
3. A book on the explanation of the names of the Prophet (peace be upon him)

Abdul Wahab "Bukhari Sahib" (born 1320 AH / 1902 CE)

Abdul Wahab "Bukhari Sahib" (born 1320 AH / 1902 CE): Though born in Hyderabad, he worked in Tamil Nadu. The history of the Arabic language in Tamil Nadu is incomplete without mentioning Bukhari Sahib, as he spent his life in various Arabic institutions in Tamil Nadu and held different positions in them. He significantly contributed to education and authorship, working as a professor and dean in various colleges in Tamil Nadu such as the Islamic College in Vaniyambadi, New College in Madras, University of Madras, and Presidency College. He finally returned to Jamalia College. He compiled his doctoral thesis on "Contribution of India to Muslim Law and Jurisprudence."

Muhammad Hasan Ali Sahib (d. 1258 AH / 1841 CE)

He hailed from the family of Hazrat Abdullah Ansari. Born as the son of Sheikh Nawazish Ali, he had opportunities to learn various Islamic and linguistic arts. He was appointed as a professor for the company in Madras in 1232 AH and was also made a Mufti, serving in these roles until his death in 1258 AH. His important works include:

1. Tabsirat al-Hikmah
2. Miftah al-Kunuz
3. Mukhtarat al-Tahrir

Muhammad Mahdi Wasif (1217 AH - 1290 AH / 1802 - 1873 CE)

Wasif was born in Madras in 1217 AH. He learned Persian from his father and Arabic from prominent scholars like Sayyid al-Qadir al-Husayni and Qadi Badr al-Dawlah, among others. He left behind significant Arabic works, including:

1. Hadiqat al-Maram
2. Tarajim
3. Firasat al-Insan fi al-Luqman

4. Tahdhib al-Akhlaq

5. Kitab fi Adab Ziyarat al-Qubur

6. Matlab al-Furqan

Dr. Syed Ali (1935 - 2003)

Dr. Syed Ali was born in Madras in 1935 as the son of Syed Yusuf, into a respected middle-class family. He earned his Master's degree in Arabic literature in 1965 from Aligarh University. He was then appointed as a lecturer in the Arabic department at New College, eventually becoming the head of this department. He continued in this role until his retirement in 1993. During his tenure, he had many opportunities to visit various Arab countries. The President of India recognized his valuable contributions to promoting Arabic language and literature in India. He significantly contributed to the dissemination of Arabic through his valuable writings, lectures, and academic seminars. His notable works include:

1. دعنا نتحدث بالعربية (Let us Converse in Arabic)

2. اللغة العربية للمبتدئين (Arabic for Beginners)

Dr. Nisar Ahmed (born 1950)

 Dr. Peshimam Nisar Ahmed was born in 1950 in the town of Vaniyambadi, Vellore district, Tamil Nadu, India. He earned his Master's degree in Arabic language and advanced Master's degree in Arabic language and his PhD from the University of Madras. With over thirty years of experience in teaching and supervising research, his valuable Arabic works include:

1. I'jaz al-Qur'an
2. Ilm al-Tafsir wa al-Hadith
3. Min Makkah al-Mukarramah ila Madras
4. Al-Fikr al-Arabi fi al-Qarn al-Ishrin
5. Al-Qamus al-Jamil (Tamil-Arabic Dictionary)

Muhammad Ismail al-Nadwi (d. 1398 AH / 1978 CE)

Sheikh Muhammad al-Nadwi al-Baqawi was a distinguished scholar, particularly in the history of relations between India and the Arab world. He was born in Melvisharam as the son of Subhan Sahib and received his early education at the Islamic High School in Melvisharam. He then joined Baqiyat al-Salihat, graduating in 1955, and subsequently enrolled at Nadwatul Ulama in

Lucknow, graduating in 1957. He later went to Egypt and worked as a professor in Egypt and Algeria for a long time. He passed away in 1978 in Algeria and was buried there. His significant contributions include:

1. Tarikh al-Salat bayn al-Hind wa al-Bilad al-Arabiyyah
2. Al-Hind al-Qadimah: Hadharatuhu wa Adyanuhu
3. Al-Mu'jam al-Arabi fi al-Hind
4. Nazarat Jadidah fi Shi'r Iqbal
5. Al-Qadiyaniyyah: 'Ard wa Tahlil

Muhammad Yusuf Kokan (1334 AH - 1410 AH / 1916 - 1990 CE)

He was born in Meenampur as the son of Muhammad Ibrahim Kokan on the 4th of November, 1916. His father was a jurist, so he received his early education from his father, learned the Quran from his mother, and Urdu from the primary school. He was appointed as a lecturer in the Department of Arabic, Persian, and Urdu at the University of Madras, eventually becoming the head of this department. After his retirement, he served as a visiting professor at Calicut University and then as the dean of the Jamalia School in Madras from 1983 to 1986. He received a prestigious award from the President of India for his significant contributions to the development of Arabic studies in India. His notable works include:

1. A'lam al-Nathr wa al-Shi'r fi al-Adab al-Arabi al-Hadith (three volumes)
2. Dawlat al-Mughul
3. Alqiratul Arabiyyah
4. Alqirathul Mufidah
5. Alarabu wa adaabuhum

Dr. Syed Rahmatullah (1364 AH - 1431 AH / 1945 - 2010 CE)

A prominent contemporary scholar known for his humility, he was born in 1945 as the son of Syed Mahmood Husaini. He studied at New College and then at the University of Madras, earning his PhD in 1991. He also received a Master's degree in English from Aligarh University in 1995. He worked for 36 years as a professor of Arabic language and literature at New College. He passed away on August 17, 2010. His contributions include works in Arabic, Urdu, and English, such as:

1. Al-Adyan (five volumes)

2. Aqdhiyat Rasul Allah (The Judgments of the Prophet Muhammad)
3. Qawa'id al-Lughah al-Arabiyyah al-Asasiyyah (Basic Arabic Grammar Rules)
4. Bughiyah li Kulli Muslim (Desire for Every Muslim)
5. Mazaaq al-'Arifin (in Urdu)

Syed Karamatullah Bahmani (born 1948)

Dr. Bahmani was born in Tambaram near Madras to Maulana Syed Sultan Mohiuddin Bahmani Sahib and Habib al-Nisa Begum in 1948. He earned the title of "Afzal al-Ulama" in Islamic and Arabic sciences from the University of Madras, a diploma in higher education, and a PhD in Arabic literature. He worked as a professor in the Arabic department at New College and as the head of Islamic studies at the University of Madras. His significant works include:

1. Kurasah al-Khatt al-Arabi (Arabic Calligraphy Workbook)
2. Khutuwat Kabirah ila al-Arabiyyah al-Wazifiyyah (Major Steps to Functional Arabic)
3. Qawa'id al-Lughah al-Arabiyyah (Arabic Grammar Rules)

Qadi Nizamuddin Ahmad al-Saghir (1113 AH - 1189 AH)

Qadi Nizamuddin was born in Arcot in 1113 AH. He studied under the teachers of his time, and after his father's death, he was appointed as Qadi (judge) and head of the government of Arcot. Along with his judicial duties, he was involved in writing, teaching, and was also interested in medicine. His notable Arabic works include:

1. Inba' al-Adhkiya bi-Tahbib al-Tayyib wa al-Nisa ila Sayyid al-Anbiya (Informing the Intelligent about the Love of Perfume and Women by the Master of Prophets)
2. Husul al-Mabarat bi-Sharh Dala'il al-Khayrat (Attainment of Blessings through the Explanation of the Guides to Good Deeds)
3. Waqa'i' Muhimmah (Important Events)

Qadi Nizamuddin Ahmad (1113 - 1189 AH): Qadi Nizamuddin Ahmad wrote the treatise titled "Inba' al-Adhkiya bi-Tahbib al-Tayyib wa al-Nisa ila Sayyid al-Anbiya" at the request of Nawab Muhammad Mahfuz Khan Bahadur. In this treatise, he explained the hadith "Love of perfume and women has been made dear to me, and my solace is in prayer." This work serves as an excellent rebuttal to Orientalists who criticize the Prophet Muhammad (PBUH) for his multiple marriages. Qadi Nizamuddin Ahmad passed away on 23 Ramadan 1189 AH in Arcot and was buried there.

Maulana Abdul Wahab al-Madrasasi (1208 - 1285 AH)

Maulana Abdul Wahab al-Madrasasi hailed from the Nawait family, known for its scholarly and religious contributions, boasting a clear history of services, heroism, glory, and pride. The distinguished scholars from this family played a significant role in the history of Islam, transforming the lives of Muslims in South India and beyond. They served Islam and Muslims with their writings and speeches in all aspects of intellectual, spiritual, social, and political life. Maulana Abdul Wahab al-Madrasasi was a prominent scholar and an adept jurist. The Nawaits are a group from Quraysh, tracing their lineage back to Muhammad (PBUH) through Nadhar bin Kinana. They migrated from Medina to Basra during the era of Hajjaj bin Yusuf al-Thaqafi and the Caliph Abu Ja'far al-Mansur. From Basra, they moved to South India in the eighth century. This renowned family, known as the Badr al-Dawla family, gained fame for producing scholars, poets, and judges.

The Nawait family flourished and remained in the hearts of rulers and leaders due to their scholarly and religious prowess and their competence in national affairs. Sheikh Abdul Hayy al-Hasani, the author of "Nuzhat al-Khawatir," mentioned Maulana Abdul Wahab al-Madrasasi as follows:

"He was of good character, high ambition, and noble disposition, knowledgeable in both worldly and religious matters. He engaged in royal services after his father's death, taking on leadership in the military in 1242 AH and assuming the ministerial role in 1254 AH. He was bestowed with grand titles."

In the year 1260 AH, Maulana Abdul Wahab al-Madrasasi retired from his duties, but the prince did not accept his resignation and instead appointed him as a representative to attend meetings with rulers to resolve disputes. He passed away on the 5th of Rabi' al-Awwal, 1285 AH. Abdul Wahab al-Madrasasi led a scholarly life full of effort in acquiring knowledge, managing administrative duties, teaching, and writing. Although involved in administrative work, he dedicated himself to writing and authored many books in Persian and Arabic. He wrote five books in Arabic and five in Persian. His Arabic works include:

1. Akmal al-Wasa'il li-Rijal al-Shama'il li-Tirmidhi (The

Best Means for the Men of the Characteristics of Tirmidhi)

2. Risalah fi 'Ilm al-Jughrafiya (Treatise on Geography)

3. Al-Kawakib al-Durriyah (The Radiant Stars) - Selected Majalis in Usul al-Fiqh

4. Kashf al-Ahwal 'an Naqd al-Rijal fi Asma' al-Du'afa (Unveiling the Conditions of Criticism of Men in the Names of the Weak)

5. Badr al-Ghurrat fi Asma' al-Qurra' al-'Asharah (The Full Moon in the Names of the Ten Reciters)

6. Kashif al-Umuzat ila al-Waraqat fi Usul al-Fiqh al-Dinawariyyah (Unveiling the Mysteries to the Paper in the Principles of Fiqh of Dinawari)

7. Sanad al-Zairin fi al-Radd 'ala al-Wahhabiyyin (Support for the Visitors in Refuting the Wahhabis)

Sheikh Muhammad Ghawth Sharaf al-Mulk Bahadur (1166 - 1238 AH)

Sheikh Muhammad Ghawth was born in Arcot in 1166 AH on a Friday night. He began his education with his grandfather Qadi Nizamuddin, studying all his schoolbooks under him. He also learned Islamic sciences from Sheikh Amin al-Din Khan. Nawab Azim al-Dawlah requested Sheikh Baqir Agha to appoint Muhammad

Ghawth as the "Diwan" (Prime Minister), which the Nawab agreed to. Muhammad Ghawth fulfilled his responsibilities with integrity and devotion. Due to his piety and excellent service, the Nawab awarded him the titles "Sharaf al-Mulk" (Honor of the Kingdom), "Sharaf al-Dawlah" (Honor of the State), and "Alam Jang" (Flag of War). However, Muhammad Ghawth did not desire to continue in his administrative role and resigned, spending the last 15 years of his life in teaching, studying, and worship. He wrote 18 books in Arabic and 13 in Persian. His Arabic works include:

1. Nathr al-Marjan fi Rasm Nazm al-Qur'an (Scattering of the Pearls in the Composition of the Qur'an)
2. Ta'liqat 'ala Sharh Qatr al-Nada (Annotations on the Explanation of Qatr al-Nada)
3. Sawati' al-Anwar fi Ma'rifat Awqat al-Salat (Illuminating Lights on Knowing the Times of Prayer)
4. Ta'liqat 'ala Mukhtasar Abi Shuja' (Annotations on the Summary of Abi Shuja')
5. Juz' fi Salat al-Tasbih (A Section on the Prayer of Glorification)
6. Kifayat al-Mubtadi fi al-Fiqh al-Shafi'i (Sufficiency for the Beginner in Shafi'i Jurisprudence)
7. Majmu'at Masa'il al-Fiqh al-Shafi'i (Collection of

Shafi'i Jurisprudence Issues)

8. Zawajir al-Irshad ila Ahl Dar al-Jihad (The Censures of Guidance to the People of the Abode of Jihad)

9. Shafi Sharh Kafi (Healing Explanation of the Sufficient)

10. Waqi'at 'Arabi (Arabic Incidents)

11. Bast al-Yadayni li-Ikram al-Abawayn (Extending the Hands in Honoring the Parents)

12. Al-Fawa'id al-Sibghiyya (The Dyed Benefits)

13. Al-Najm al-Waqad fi Sharh Qasidat Banat Su'ad (The Fiery Star in Explaining the Poem Banat Su'ad)

14. Nawazir al-Fara'id wa Buhur al-Fara'id (The Rare Gems of Obligations and the Seas of Obligations)

15. Kafi Mukhtasar Kafiya (Sufficient Summary of the Sufficient)

16. Arjuzah fi Alqab Hadrat Amir al-Mu'minin Ali bin Abi Talib (Poem on the Titles of Hadrat Amir al-Mu'minin Ali bin Abi Talib)

17. Rasa'il al-Barakat fi Sharh Dala'il al-Khairat (Letters of Blessings in Explaining the Guide of Good Deeds)

18. Hawashi 'ala al-Qamus (Marginalia on the Dictionary)

Sheikh Muhammad Sibghatullah Qadi Badr al-Dawla

Sheikh Qadi Badr al-Dawla was born on 5 Muharram 1211

AH in Madras. He studied under Maulana Abdul Ali Bahr al
-Ulum for the science of morphology as a blessing and
under Maulvi Ja'far Hussain for morphology and grammar.
He learned Usul al-Fiqh, philosophy, theology, and logic
under Maulana Ala al-Din, the king of scholars. For the
remaining traditional and rational sciences, he studied
under his father, Maulana Muhammad Ghawth Sharaf al-
Mulk Bahadur. Qadi Badr al-Dawla did not just study the
regular curriculum but also read various books on diverse
sciences and arts available during his time. He authored
29 books in Arabic and 23 in Persian. His Arabic works
include:

Major Works:

1. Risala fi Siyam Sitta Shawwal
2. Al-Arba'in fi Mu'jizat Sayyid al-Mursalin
3. Rashq al-Siham ila Man Dha'if Kullu Muskhar
   Haram
4. Fahras Ahadith Ma'jam al-Saghir
5. Hidayat al-Salik li-Muwatta' Imam Malik
6. Hawashi Kitab al-Muntaqa
7. Hawashi Sahih Muslim
8. Risala fi al-Khidhab
9. Risala fi Tahreem al-Mut'ah
10. Nur al-'Ayn fi Manaqib al-Husayn (RA)
11. Risala Sughra fi al-Siyar wa al-Manaqib

12. Risala Kubra fi al-Siyar wa al-Manaqib

13. Al-Maktubat bi-al-'Arabiyya

14. Dhail 'ala al-Qawl al-Musaddad fi al-Dhib 'an Musnad al-Imam Ahmad

15. Al-Matali' al-Badriyyah Sharh al-Kawkab al-Durri

16. Risala fi Tahqiq al-Salat al-Wusta

17. Al-Tariq fi Dar al-Mariq

18. Risala fi I'rab al-Rabb fi "Allahumma Rabb hadhihi al-Da'wat al-Tamma"

19. Hikayat Luqman

20. Risala fi Ta'yin Sadaq Fatimah al-Zahra (RA)

21. Umda al-Ra'id fi Funun al-Fara'id

22. Risala fi Ta'lim al-Nisa' al-Kitabah

23. Sharh Hashiyat Sharh Mawaqif

Prominent Prose Writings of Tamil Nadu

Tamil Nadu's Contributions to Arabic Prose

The state of Tamil Nadu has given birth to a considerable number of scholars, writers, jurists, Hadith scholars, and interpreters whose reputation has spread throughout the Islamic world thanks to their valuable works. Some of these works have become foundational in Islamic and Arabic arts. The Arabic language has been studied and learned in this state as the language of Islamic studies, and scholars and writers have devoted great effort to preserving, disseminating, and developing it across Tamil Nadu.

Thanks to these scholars and writers, Tamil Nadu has produced remarkable works in scientific, religious, linguistic, and literary subjects, some of which rival the works of prominent Arab writers.

Factors contributing to this activity and development include the establishment of religious schools, Arabic colleges, Islamic institutes, and universities across the state, along with the proliferation of printing presses and the publication of Arabic journals and magazines. These factors have led to a proliferation of Arabic books, both literary and scientific, with more than a hundred such works being produced. Therefore, this space cannot accommodate the mentioning of their titles and authors.

Here, we will focus on reviewing those Arabic books that have been written on various subjects and enjoy significant acceptance and fame in Tamil Nadu and beyond.

(1) History

1. أعلام النثر والشعر في العصر العربي الحديث

This book, authored by Sheikh Muhammad Yusuf Kokan Al-Umri, chronicles the history of contemporary and modern Arabic literature in the Arabian Peninsula, Egypt, Iraq, Syria, and Lebanon, highlighting the Arabs' scientific, religious, literary achievements, and their literary works.

2. العرب وآدابهم

The Arabs and Their Literature: Also authored by Professor Muhammad Yusuf Kokan Al-Umri, this valuable book consists of two parts: the first part containing 120 pages and the second part containing

178 pages. These two parts elucidate the civilization of the Arabian Peninsula from the pre-Islamic era to the present.

Arabic Prose Works:

١ . دولة المغول في الهند

The Mongol Empire in India: Authored by Professor Muhammad Yusuf Kokan Al-Umri, this book delves into the governance of Muslim Mongol rulers in India over 332 years, examining their political situations and issues. It spans 270 pages.

١. تاريخ الصلات بين الهند و البلاد العربية

The History of Relations Between India and Arab Lands: Written by Dr. Muhammad Ismail Al-Nadawi Al-Baqawi, this book discusses the historical, cultural, political, intellectual, scientific, and literary relations between India and Arab lands through the ages without bias, focusing on their mutual achievements.

٢. الهند القديمة : حضاراتها ودياناتها

Ancient India: Its Civilizations and Religions: Also authored by Sheikh Muhammad Ismail Al-Nadawi Al-Baqawi, this book, published in 1970 by Dar Al-Shaab in Cairo, provides a detailed comparative study of literature, religions, history, and philosophy in ancient India, shedding light on its civilization, culture, and traditions.

3. الفكر العربي في القرن العشرين

Arab Thought in the Twentieth Century: Dr. Peshimam Nisar Ahmed authored this book, which discusses the societal conditions in the Arab world and the emergence of new ideas in the twentieth century, such as Arab nationalism, socialism, democracy, and Islamic movements, analyzing their causes and the resulting changes in Arab countries in detail.

Grammar:

1. القراءة المفيدة: Divided into two parts, the first part containing 72 pages and the second part containing 178 pages, this book, authored by Professor Muhammad Yusuf Kokan Al-Umri, is designed for students aspiring to learn Arabic. The author has written it in a modern and easy-to-understand style to facilitate learning.

Educational Texts in Tamil Nadu:

1. القراءة العربية: Authored by Professor Muhammad Yusuf Kokan, this book spans 176 pages and is designed for school and college students. It covers moral lessons and Islamic teachings in a simple and easy-to-understand style, receiving wide acceptance and admiration in Arabic schools, colleges, technical institutes, and Islamic centers in India.

2. Mirqat Al-Nahw: Written by Sheikh Shah Al-Hameed, known as "Sahib Al-Jalwa" (d. 1920 CE), this book is a clear exposition of Arabic grammar titled "Mirqat Al-Nahw." Its lessons aid beginner students in learning Arabic, and it is part of the curriculum in most Arabic schools in Tamil Nadu.

3. دروس اللغة العربية لغير الناطقين بها

Arabic Language Lessons for Non-Native Speakers: Dr. V. Abdul Rahim authored this three-part book to facilitate Arabic language learning for beginners. It contains lessons covering various modern sciences and arts, presented in a simple and straightforward style. Although beneficial, this book does not replace newer publications from Arab countries. It was printed multiple times by the Islamic Foundation in Chennai.

4. قواعد النحوية العربية

Arabic Grammar Rules: Authored by Professor Syed

Karamatullah Bahmani, this book aims to simplify basic Arabic grammar rules for Arabic language students. It covers essential grammatical rules according to different lessons. Notably, half of the book is in Arabic and the other half in English, making it suitable for students in schools, colleges, universities, and institutes across Tamil Nadu, as well as in Assam, Andhra Pradesh, and other regions.

5.المسعف في لغة وإعراب سورة يوسف

This book was prepared by Dr. V. Abdul Rahim. It is one of the finest books that gained fame in India in the twentieth century. This book comprises 212 pages, aiming to explain and clarify the rules of Arabic language and grammar in Surah Yusuf.

6. نصوص من الحديث النبوي الشريف

This book was compiled by Mr. V. Abdul Rahim and it includes Arabic grammatical issues and rules with the collection of 16 Hadiths. This book contains 123 pages and it was printed by the printing house "Dar Al-Bashir" in Jordan.

(c) Biographies

1. الأبيات المقدسة

Sacred Verses: Thirukkural is a lengthy poem in the Tamil language borrowed by the famous poet "Thiruvalluvar" in the third century AD. Each couplet consists of two short lines, with four parts in the first line and three parts in the second line. Though there are limitations in terms of poetic expressions, the poet excels in three important subjects: ethics, internal politics, and sexual sciences. Sheikh Mohammed Yousuf Kokan Al-Umri translated the entire poem into Arabic.

2.الحزب الأفخم منتقبة الغوث الأعظم

This book was authored by Sheikh Moulavi Mufti Mahmood (died 1934). He outlined the biography of Sheikh Abdul Qadir Gilani. His style is characterized by clarity of expression, detailing the important aspects of Sheikh Abdul Qadir Gilani's life.

3. خليل مطران

Khalil Mataran: This book was written by Mr. Mohammed Yousuf Kokan Al-Umri, shedding light on the life of Khalil Mataran. It presents a wonderful and realistic portrayal of Khalil Mataran's life, including his news, events, and writings. This book consists of 73 published pages.

(d) Islamic Sciences

1. أهم المهمات

Important Missions: This book was authored by Sheikh Tekiya Ahmed Abdul Qadir, known as "Sheikh Naykam" (died 1976), who explained some religious matters with a clear and simple style. This book addresses important religious issues in an easy and clear manner, and it has gained the admiration of readers and researchers in Islamic sciences.

2. الحقائق الأساسية في الديانة الإسلامية

Basic Facts in the Islamic Religion: This book is authored by Dr. Abdul Halim Muhammad Saeed. The book explains the concepts and principles of the Islamic religion in a smooth and clear manner, making it an important reference in the study of Islamic sciences.

3. المنهاج الإسلامي

Islamic Model: A book by Sheikh Abdul Qadir bin Muhammad Al-Madani, addressing topics of creed, jurisprudence, and Islamic ethics, making it an important book in the curriculum for Islamic sciences in Tamil Nadu.

4. السيرة النبوية الشريفة

The Noble Biography of the Prophet: A book containing the biography of Prophet Muhammad, authored by Sheikh Muhammad Yousuf Kokan Al-Umri. The book covers important events and milestones in the life of Prophet Muhammad, and it has garnered praise from readers and researchers.

5. الصلوات القرآنية

Quranic Prayers: This book was authored by Qazi Ubaidullah (1927). It is one of the most famous works on the subject of the Quran. Sheikh Ubaidullah exerted tremendous efforts in this work.

6 . في بلاد هرقل

In the Land of Heraclius: This book was written by Dr. V. Abdul Rahim. It discusses the dialogue in which Abu Sufyan ibn Harb, may Allah be pleased with him, narrates his visit to Heraclius in his land.

7. التنبيه بالتنزيه

The Attention with Distinction: Sheikh Moulavi Mufti Mahmood Said (1247 - 1312 AH) authored this book for those interested in Islam and its rules, especially those contrary to the opinions of Sheikh Imam Ibn Taymiyyah and his followers. This book consists of 436 pages divided into an introduction, seven chapters, and a conclusion. It was printed by the "Mahboob Shahi" printing press in Hyderabad.

8. تشنيد المباني في تخريج أحاديث مكتوبات إمام رباني

Structuring Buildings in Graduating Narrations of the Guiding Imam: Sheikh Moulavi Mufti Mahmood Said authored this book. It contains 120 pages and was printed by the "Fayd Al-Karim" printing press in Hyderabad in 1311 AH.

(9)أحاديث سهلة

 Easy Hadiths: This book was authored by Dr. V. Abdul Rahim. Sheikh Rahim selected 20 Hadiths and provided detailed explanations for them. This book was published by the Islamic Foundation Trust, Chennai.

(10)الحج والعمرة والزيارة

Hajj, Umrah, and Visitation: This book was authored by Dr. V. Abdul Rahim, the former head of the Arabic Language Department for Non-Native Speakers at the Islamic University in Medina. He received an appreciation award from the President of India for his contribution to the dissemination of the Arabic language in India. This book is very famous as it mentions the rituals of Hajj and how to perform them in beautiful and simple expressions.

(11)الروضة المكللة في الأحاديث المسلسلة:

The Decorated Garden of Continuous Hadiths: This book was compiled by Qazi Ubaidullah (1927). It contains 251 pages.

(12)الصلوات الطيبات على خير البريات

Good Prayers for the Best of Creations: This book was prepared by Qazi Ubaidullah, a renowned scholar and distinguished writer in the twentieth century. It was compiled for the benefit of seekers, as it contains many supplications, invocations, and prayers, as well as useful information for those on the path of Allah.

(13)السلك المعظم على الدر المنظم

The Honorable Path on the Organized Pearl: This book was prepared by Professor Moulavi Mufti Mahmood bin Qazi Badr al-Dawla (1934). It contains valuable annotations on "The Organized Pearl" by Sheikh Hafiz Muhammad Mazhar Naqshbandi. This book was printed by the "Best Printing Press" in Madras in 1324 AH.

14)) أكمل الوسائل لرجال الشمائل الترمذي

This book was authored by Maulana Abdul Wahab al-Madrasi. It includes the biographies of narrators, starting with the life of the venerable Imam Tirmidhi due to his compilation of "Virtuous Traits." Maulana Abdul Wahab compiled the narrators of Tirmidhi and researched them in this book, which consists of 198 pages and was printed by the "Navakl Kishore" printing press in Lucknow, divided into five chapters.

15)) الحواشي على البيضاوي والدر المنثور

Annotations on Al-Baydawi and Al-Durr Al-Munthoor: Sheikh Sadaqatullah Appa wrote explanations for Quranic Arabic books such as "Anwar al-Tanzil" and "Asrar al-Ta'weel" by Imam Al-Baydawi, completed in the year 685 AH (1286 AD), which are among the most important books of Quranic exegesis. Sheikh Sadaqatullah provided annotations to clarify difficult expressions and words. He also wrote annotations for the interpretation of "Al-Durr Al-Munthoor" by Sheikh Jalal al-Din al-Suyuti (849 AH - 1505 AD).

(16)سواطع الأنوار في معرفة أوقات الصلوة والأسحار

The Radiant Beacons in Knowing the Times of Prayer and Pre-Dawn Meals: This book was authored by Sheikh Muhammad Ghawth Sharaf al-Mulk Bahadur. The Sheikh organized it into an introduction and three chapters called "The Radiant Beacons in Knowing the Times of Prayer and Pre-Dawn Meals." This treatise consists of ninety pages, with thirteen lines on each page. The first chapter focuses on determining prayer times, the second chapter on defining celestial constellations and their depiction, and the third chapter on the hours of day and night and determining the times of night.

(17)التراث العربي في ولاية تامل نادو الهندية

 Arab Heritage in Tamil Nadu, India: This book was authored by Dr.K M A Ahamed Zubair from the New College and was published in the year 2015. It explores the Arab settlement and the spread of Islam in Tamil Nadu, as well as the development of ancient and modern Arabic poetry and the contribution of Tamil Nadu scholars to Arabic prose. It also discusses rare and exquisite manuscripts found in Tamil Nadu libraries.

Bibliography

Al-Attas, S. M. N. (1993). Islam and secularism. Kuala Lumpur: ISTAC.

Al-Dimasyqi, A.-I. A.-N. (2016). Syarh Shahih Muslim. Dar al-Kutub al-`Ilmiyah.

Allen, C. (2013). Islamophobia. In Islamophobia. https://doi.org/10.4324/9781315745077-41

al-Maraghi, M. (2002). Tafsir al-Maraghi. Beirut: Darul Fikir.

Al-Qaradawi, Y. (2010). Islam an introduction. Kuala Lumpur: Islamic Book Trust.

al-Qurtubi, A. A. M. ibn A. (2014). Tafsir al-Qurtubi (Vol. 20). Beirut: Dar al-Kutub al-'Ilmiyah.

Al-Qushayri, I. (2018). Tafsir al-Qushayri. Dar Ihya' al-Turath al-Arabi.

Al-Rāzī, F. (2000). Al-Tafsīr al-Kabīr aw Mafātih al-Gayb, Vol. VII. Dar Al-Hadith.

Al-Sya'rawi, A.-I. A.-M. (2007). Tafsir Al-Sya'rawi. Qitha' al-Saqafah wa al-Kutub.

Al-Syawkani, M. bin A. (2014). Fath al-Qadir al-Jami' baina Fannai al-Riwayah wa al-Dirayah min 'Ilm al-Tafsir, Vol. 5. Dar Ibnu Hazim.

Al-Thabathaba'i. (1987). Tafsir Al-Mizan. Islamic Publications Office.

Al-Zuhaily, W. (2009). Al-Tafsir al-Munir fi al-Aqidah wa al-Syariah wa al-Manhaj. Dar al-Fikr.

APS (Applied Social Psychology). (2017). The Role of Religion in Prejudice Enablement and Reduction. Retrieved December 26, 2022, from https://sites.psu.edu/aspsy/2017/09/28/the-role-of-religion-in-prejudice-enablement-and-reduction/

Bakhshi Hazrat 'Alī Aḥmed and Rizwānur Raḥmān. (2012). Glimpses of the Holy Qur'ān. (New Delhi: Adam Publishers and Distributors).

Chelini-Pont, B. (2013). Relationship between Stereotyping and the Place of Religion in the Public Sphere. In J. Svartvik, Jesper & Wiren (Ed.), Religious Stereotyping and Interreligious Relations (pp. 75–84). Palgrave Macmillan.

Geertz, C. (1977). The Interpretation of Cultures. Basic Books.

Geertz, C. (2013). Religion as a cultural system. In Anthropological Approaches to the Study of Religion (pp. 1–46). https://doi.org/10.4324/9781315017570

Hanafi, H. (2000). Islam in the modern world: Religion, ideology and development vol. I. Cairo: Dar Kabaa.

Hanafi, H. (2006). Culture and civilizations, conflict or dialogue? Vol. I the meridian thought. Cairo: Book Center for Publishing.

Jafari, F. (2020). Theological knowledge in Islamic mysticism and gnosticism." Kanz Philosophia A Journal for Islamic Philosophy and Mysticism 6(2). DOI: https://doi.org/10.20871/kpjipm.v6i2.92.

Karama, M. J., & Khater, N. A. (2020). Educational peace theory in the holy qur'an. Al-Bayān – Journal of Qur'ān and Ḥadīth Studies, 18, 138–154. http://scholar.ppu.edu/bitstream/handle/12345678

9/2214/1.pdf?sequence=1&isAllowed=y

Khairulnizam, M., & Saili, S. (2009). Inter-faith dialogue: The qur'anic and prophetic perspective. Journal of Usuluddin, 9(2), 65–94.

Khaldun, I. (2015). Muqaddimah. Cairo: Dar-Ibnu al-Aitam.

Kidwai, Salim. (1996). Hindustani Mufassirein Awr Unki' Arabi Tafsirein (in Urdu) .(New Delhi:Maktaba Jamiah).

Kokan, Moḥammad Yousuf. (1960). Arabic and Persian in Carnatic, (Madras: Hafiza House).

Ma'roof M M M. (1995). *Spoken Tamil dialect of the Muslims of Sri Lanka: Language as Identity classifier*. Islamic Studies 34 (4).

Nashir, H. (2015). Understanding the ideology of Muhammadiyah. Muhammadiyah University Press.

Nieuwkerk, K. van, LeVine, M., & Stokes, M. (2016). Islam and popular culture. University of Texas Press.

Patji, A. R. (1991). The Arabs of Surabaya: a study of sociocultural integration. Canberra: Australian

National University.

Putra, A. D., Purnomo, D., & Utomo, A. W. (2019). Sociological study of harmony in diversity: Lessons from Salatiga. Walisongo: Jurnal Penelitian Sosial Keagamaan, 27(1), 69–98. 10.21580/ws.27.1.3504

Ridwan, M., & Robikah, S. (2019). Ethical vision of the qur'an: Interpreting concept of the qur'anic sociology in developing religious harmony. Jurnal Ilmiah Islam Futura, 18(2), 308–326. http://dx.doi.org/10.22373/jiif.v19i2.5444

Sanaa Sha'lan, 'Adore Me'(A'shaquni), Daira al-Maktaba al- Wataniyya, Hashemite Kingdom of Jordan, Third Edition, 2016.

Saerozi, M. (2017). Dynamics of the development of istiqomah mosque in front of a church in Ungaran Central Java Indonesia. Journal of Indonesian Islam, 11(02), 423–458. 10.15642/JIIS.2017.11.2.423-458

Saged, A. A. (2021). Honoring the human self with a world peace study in the light of purposes the holy quran. Quranika: Journal of Libahuts Qur'an, 19(2), 223–234.

Shareef, Moḥammed Muṣṭafa and Bad'iuddin Ṣabri. (2008). Development of Tafseer Literature in India, (Hyderabad: Osmania University).

Shihab, M. Q. (2004). Tafsir al-mishbah. Jakarta: Lentera Hati.

Shu'aib, Tayka. (1993). Arabic, Arwi and Persian in Sarandib and Tamil Nadu, (Chennai: Imaamul Aroos Trust).

Thabari, I. J. (1999). Tafsir al Thabari. Kairo: Dar al Fikr.

Zamakhsyari, M. I. U. al. (2012). Al-kassyaf 'an haqaiq al-tanzil wa 'uyun al-ta'wil fi wujuh al-ta'wil. Cairo: Dar al-Hadis.

Zubair, K M A Aḥamed. (2010). *Tamil-Arabic Relationship*, ed. John Samuel G, (Chennai:The Institute of Asian Studies Press).

Zubair, K M A Ahamed. (2012). *Eminent Scholars of Sheik Sadaqathullah Appa's Family and their contribution to Arabic and Islamic Studies,* (in Arabic), Thaqafatul ḥind 54, (3&4).

Zubair, K M A Ahamed. (2013). *Qasaid al-Madaih al-Nabaviyya fi Tamil Nadu,* (in Arabic), Thaqafatul ḥind 64, (4).

Zubair, K M A Aḥamed. (2017). Prophet's Panegyrics in Arabic Literature, (Moldova: Lambert Academic Publishing).